Those Days, These Days

A Poetry Collection

Copyright © 2021 Hannah Edge

All rights reserved. This book or any portion thereof may not be reproduced or used in any manner whatsoever without the express written permission of the publisher except for the use of brief quotations in a book review or scholarly journal.

Published by Llais Newydd Poetry Press

First Edition: 2021

ISBN 9798555242907

About the Author

My name is Riven Stellan, and I'm from a small coastal town in South Africa. Life wasn't easy growing up—I left school early and faced the harsh realities of poverty. Despite the challenges, I built a career in the automotive industry, earning international certification through determination and hard work.

Writing has always been a passion of mine. In my youth, I expressed my emotions through poems and short stories, using them as an outlet to make sense of the world around me. Over time, the pressures of life dulled that creative spark, but not too long ago, something inside me changed. I felt an overwhelming need to channel my personal feelings and frustrations into stories—stories that could connect with others who might be going through similar struggles.

I love crafting gripping narratives, ones that pull you in and make you live in the moment. When a story touches something deep inside, when it strikes a nerve or feels relatable—that's when it truly matters to me. My writing focuses on emotion, on creating characters and experiences that feel real. I aim to craft moments that help readers step into someone else's shoes, to feel what they feel, and to maybe find strength in those connections.

For me, writing is more than just storytelling—it's a way to inspire, to offer understanding, and to remind us all, that we're not alone in our struggles.

Read more at https://rstellan24.my.canva.site/.

Milton Keynes UK
Ingram Content Group UK Ltd.
UKHW022127291124
451915UK00010B/564

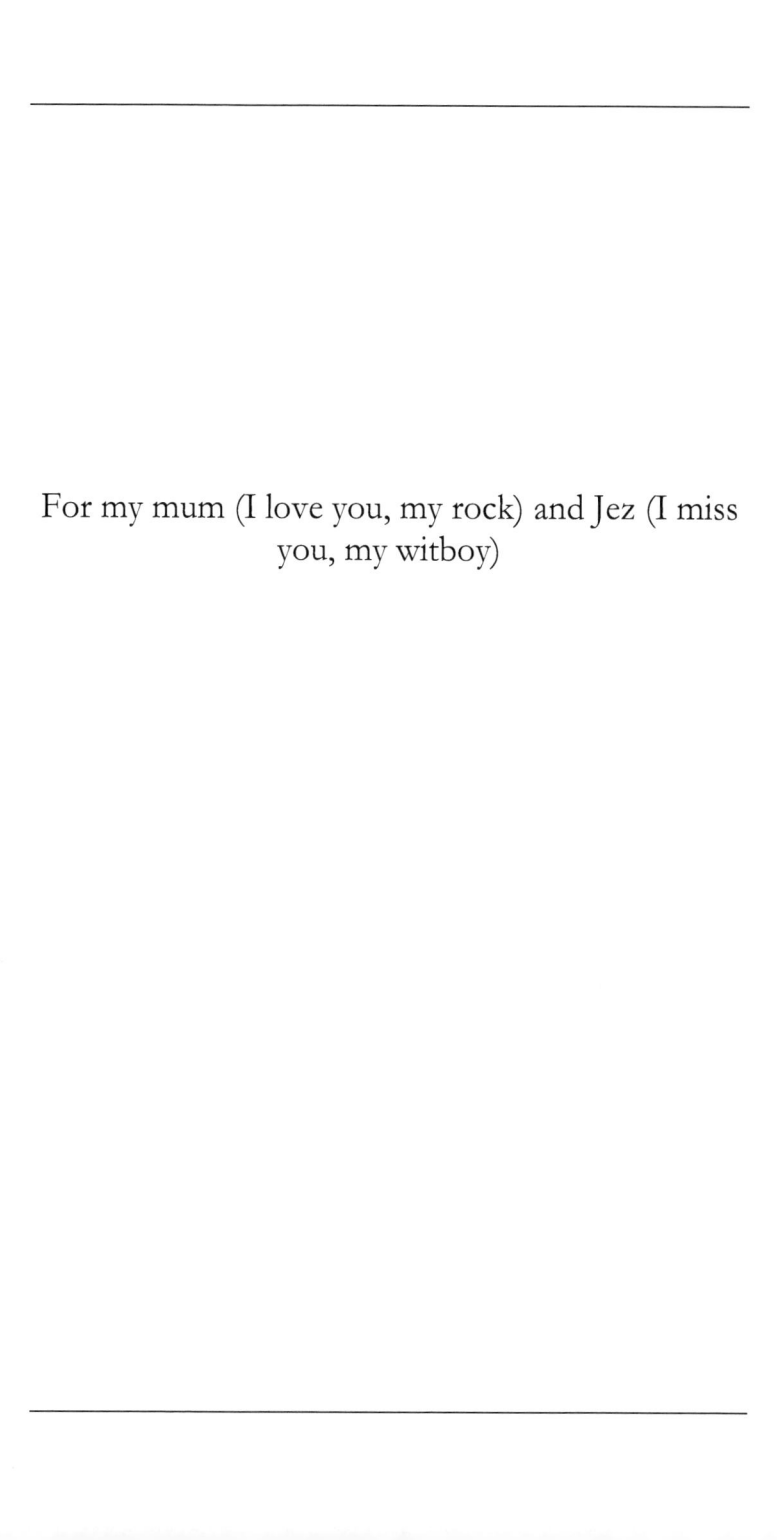

For my mum (I love you, my rock) and Jez (I miss you, my witboy)

Acknowledgements

Wow. So, this is actually happening. It's no longer a distant pipe-dream. I have a few important people that deserve to be thanked for helping me with this collection, and also for helping me 'be me' and survive my tribulations.

So, firstly, Mum. Without your support for the last thirty-plus years, I wouldn't be here, and this collection wouldn't exist. From the age of 6, when I first started writing, you have encouraged my passion. You supported me through my tough teen years and embraced me for who I am. I can honestly say, I wouldn't be here without you, and I wouldn't be my true self. Thank you, thank you, thank you.

Secondly, to the best step-dad in the world. Davie, you are a dude of a dad. Always ready with a rude or silly limerick whenever I say I'm stuck on a poem. Always able to make me chuckle even when I'm grumpy or in my own crazy little world. You love me like your own, never questioned my quirks, never cared if I was gay. I couldn't have asked for a better dad.

Dee Dickens. Mate. You, my dear, are incredible. You are my publisher, editor, friend and mentor. You pick me up when I'm low, you fill me with compliments and self-belief, you encourage me to be me. Every bone in your body is filled with kindness, and I genuinely feel like I've won the lottery having such a friend. You re-lit the poetic fire in my belly. You re-opened the door into the poetry community. You have had such an insane impact on me and my life.

Joe Thomas. We started out by bonding over cute Nintendo animals. I never dreamed that within a few short, 2020-crazy months, you would become my editor and publisher. You are an incredible writer and a gorgeous person. I am so grateful for your friendship and constant compliments. You inspire me, dude, big time.

Gavin. Gav. Gavonius. What a man! All 6ft 4in of you! You taught me the meaning of 'gentle giant'. You taught me to feel safe around men. No partner has ever been able to peel back my writing curtain. No partner has ever been allowed to stick in their two cents. Until you. And boy, do I love your two cents! Thank you for your help during the editing process of this little beast. Thank you for being quiet when I'm on Zoom talking poetry with my friends. Thank you for understanding that I'm not your average woman. You love my queerness, you love my quirkiness. You love me for me. I don't think you realise how unusual that is to find in a person. I love you, my gorgeous daf' twat.

Stacey. Mate. You have spent two (yes *two*) decades listening to me waffle about literally everything, but mostly football (seriously, I've had a good look around, no one else has managed this!). You pick me up when I'm at my lowest. You have pulled me back from the cliff edge more times than I care to count. You supported me through all my confusion over what the heck was 'wrong' with me. You gave a damn, you give a damn. I will be eternally grateful for that support… even if you do support City!

Sally. My adorable buddy. Without you, I would never have known I am autistic. Despite all your struggles, you have always dropped everything to help me. Your intellect would intimidate me, if I didn't know how oblivious you are to your own genius and beauty. I promise, when we're older, I'm well up for crazy blue rinses and clinking bags of tinned cat food; Eleanor Abernathy eat yer 'eart out!

I've made some really beautiful friendships this year and I want to give a shout out to those people too. Noah, spawn of Dee, you are an incredible person. Your determination to ensure everyone feels loved is inspirational. Your kindness knows no bounds, and makes me feel loved, liked and happy. Josefine, such a sweet, gentle, caring friend and amazing poet. You're stuck with me now duck! Louisa, for proving I'm not the only person in this country that is obsessed with Neighbours! For keeping me sane and in-the-know during lockdown. You could have told me to bugger off, it was your downtime, but you didn't. My Tyneside doppelgänger! Everybody at Roath Writers, you have been inspirational. You welcomed me with big, open arms and made me feel part of your amazing family. You have all had an impact on me and my writing, thank you.

And lastly, because of the amount of struggles I've had over the years, I want to thank myself. Cheesy, I know. But it's important. I spent so long ill, unhappy, not writing. If I'd looked at myself, even just 6 months ago, and seen I was this far down my personal road, I would have laughed it off as another delusion. It wasn't. Hannah, you worked really bloody hard, and literally changed your life and how you look at yourself. I'm proud of you and what you have accomplished!

Table of Contents

Introduction 1

Back Garden Goodbyes 4

You're The One That I Want 6

Shark-Infested Garden 7

Daisy Chain 8

Tomboy 10

Anticipated Adolescence 12

Addictive Rebellion 13

The First Dance 14

Hello Silkmen 16

A Brief History 18

Shh 19

Keeping Mum 21

Coming Out 23

A Northern Changing Room 24

An Ode 25

Law Be Damned 27

Keep It Under Wraps 29

Pride 30

Those Days 32

(Not) Our Fight 35

Watch And Pray 36

Goodbye Silkmen 37

Caus-Tic 39

In The Darkness 41

Forest Hands 42

Autistic Sensibilities 44

Beauty in the Beast 46

Less Judging 48

To Your Right 49

Impossible Politics 50

Silicon Era 51

Flight 53

Forsaken 54

Crown of Thorns 56

These Days 57

About the author 59

Introduction

Hello Reader!

Welcome to the world of me! I've finally gone and done it, after years of procrastination and lack of self-belief! This collection is all poetry; it is dark in places, but you will come to see the positivity and optimism that oozes from my every pore.

Part One, Those Days, takes you on my childhood journey. This was a time when homosexuality was still frowned upon in Britain, when it induced hatred and violence. The 90s, when it was still illegal for a teacher to show support to a young, gay kid. I had a mouth on me, I wasn't afraid to speak up. These poems are a reflection of those struggles.

Part Two, These Days, takes you on a mixed journey. Through my struggles with anxiety, which were later identified as symptoms of my autism. Through my liberal, equalist eyes as I watch the world rapidly implode. Through 2020 and the sheer craziness of it all.

There is a vein, that runs through this collection. Sport. Sport has kept me sane; it makes me bounce with joy. When I watch a game, no matter what sport, I see artistry. I want you to experience that. If you're not a sports lover, I hope you will see that this passion is transferable to whatever *your* passion is.

Though your struggles may have been different to mine, we have all had tough times. I hope this collection helps you to see you can be who you are, other's be damned. I hope you see that there is always light at the end of the tunnel.

Enjoy my friends!

Those Days

Back Garden Goodbyes

I remember the swing of the axe
as we stood watching
his muscles flex, his beard twitch,
sweat in a 'v' on his chest.

I remember hopping from one foot
to the other, rubbing hands
together, a cacophony of glee
and laughter left our throats.

I remember he stopped
to ask where my trainers were
as I wiggled my toes in the warm grass,
skin of my heels on the skin of our Earth.

He made a notch in the tree,
pale, fresh, new-born wood -
a fissure breaking through
wizened bark.

Like a golfer judging his swing,
as the ball rests on its tee
ready for take-off,
he swung.

He hacked, hewed, mopped his brow;
hacked, hewed, kneaded aching shoulders.

As it fell, the ground trembling
through my soles to my soul,
Porgie's coffin groaned.

And I swear I felt her twitch

beneath me.

You're The One That I Want

Joe, my brother's Action Man,
has to watch from the sidelines
unless I can dress him in Barbie's skirt.

Ken struts his stuff, shirt half open,
hair gelled back like Danny Zuko,
smirking at jealous Joe.

Barbie, all dolled up in her new
lurid, pink jacket, winks like Rizzo
at Ken *and* Joe. My brother cackles,
disarms his army doll, dresses him in the skirt.

Big Sis' wins: Jo marries Barbie,
ignoring Cindy's muffled cries
from the box of unwanted toys.

Shark-Infested Garden

Daddy takes a saw to every tree.
Leaves their stumps
for me to stand on. Hopping
from one to the next.

Teeter with me,
feel the wind
against your cheeks,
hair blowing into our eyes.

Look down at the turquoise and grey –
a churning, frothing ocean. Fins slice
through choppy water, encircling us.

Noses rise
from the rippling water.
Their gaping jaws close in,
bright white daggers
sharp teeth
seeking our innocent flesh.

Dusk air clips our chin,
the moon crackles through our vision
calling 'time' on perilous fun.

See the grass, inches below,
waiting patiently for tomorrow's game.

Daisy Chain

We met at the after-school book club,
two geeks in a pod.
When she spoke, I was rapt;
watching her talk with her hands,
gesturing enthusiasm for Mallory Towers;
seeing her talk with her eyes,
how they sparkled for Anastasia Krupnik.

Too young to understand
why I needed to be near her.
I wanted, so badly,
to invite her for tea,
share my toys,
show her the books I slept with -
my paper-scented teddy bears.

Primal instinct prodded me,
discouraged me, as though it knew
this wasn't normal.
A sandpit of confusion.
A tummy of worms and butterflies,
ladybirds and dragonflies.
My throat, a gobstopper lump

as we sit, at the back
of the school field,
shaded by evergreen pines,
the screeching of happy, football-playing
kids floating by on the wind.
She talked about why George
was better than Dick or Julian.

I plucked daisies, and pierced holes

in their stems with nimble
8 year old fingers,
threaded daisy into daisy,
quietly wrapped the chain
around her wrist.

Tomboy

Summer freedom of copying the Karate Kid;
a ring made of shoes and t-shirts.
I stand, skinny arms raised,
fierce scowl on my face
as the boy-next-door yells *ding*.

You watch from the side,
plaster-casted arm waving,
fist clenched, nonsensical cheers
from your mouth as I pound
my victim to a pretend pulp.

The boy-next-door pulls me off
my prone brother, shouts *time*;
Arms raised victorious, I dance
around the home-made ring.

You guide me away, sweaty hand
in sweaty hand; away from the field,
my trainers, the safety of my brother.
You compliment my uppercuts
and Naseem-esque weaving.

We sit on playground woodchip,
damp from summer rain.
Bottom numb, arms goosebumpy,
ear tickled from the puppy-soft fuzz
on your upper lip.

Six months I've made you wait.
I wanted Solksjaer or Ryan Giggs.
Not a Northern Minirat gangster,
with a stolen bike and a broken arm.

I sit fidgeting, trying to think
of something other than football.
You sit fidgeting, trying to cajole
me by stroking my leg.

So I let you kiss me
on the cheek.

Anticipated Adolescence

In a secret glade behind my house,
away from mum's earshot -
you tear a branch from a nearby tree.

The copse emptied with gangster
threats: your attempt at romance.
Relationship of hand-holding,
cheek-kissing, bike-riding adoration.

We sit on the baking hot, dusty ground,
not knowing what to say.
You use the twig as a pen
in the dry, grey earth.

I love you.
My tummy flips,
like when you reach the peak
of Blackpool's Pepsi Max ride
and plummet.
I love you too.

Addictive Rebellion

It started with a cigar -
me and Lee hid under a tree,
a shaking hand full of matches.
No wind, just the scratch
against the box. A flickering
orange flame warmed my fingertips.
It was awful.

So he stole a cigarette
from his dad's secret stash.
Back to the tree, it lit
easily with a little sizzle
from the Rizla. Lee coughed,
spluttered, passed it

to me. My lungs filled
like on bonfire night
in the shade of autumn's
heat. The taste of parkin
and treacle teased my tongue.
I groaned; lips curled
with a knowing smile.

The First Dance
An Ode To Basketball Legend, Michael Jordan

They gifted me a TV,
so huge it covered my dresser,
so deep I could use it as another shelf
for my ornamental cats and plastic trolls;
so deep my cat could stretch out,
drape his paws casually over the top
and still not knock over the aerial.

My brand new, second-hand TV,
early technicolour and Dolby surround sound.
You tuned in the channels
by twiddling a plastic knob
like you still get on old car radios.

Turn with tweaks - the vast screen
of black and white pixels dancing, crackling,
vibrating through the plastic sides.

Turn with a twitch - a tease
of colour. Flash of orange,
long red streaks, flitting side to side.

Crackling becomes commentary.
And Rodman passes to Jordan.
A picture emerges, the magic
of finely tuned pixels
turns dots into men

and I see you
as you dance across my screen;
the ball, dribbled gracefully,
connected to you.

You soar like Icarus,
smash the ball through the net,
swing from its lip,
and land like Daedalus.

I stand frozen, transfixed
by your smile as you celebrate,
as you disappear under a sea
of elated, red-clothed Bulls.

Hello Silkmen

Still small enough to duck
under the rusty turnstile,
its coat of blue paint
now just a suggestion.

Through the cavernous tunnel,
tangled in a throng
of grown men sporting
blue and white scarves,
replica shirts stretched
over beer bellies.
I smell stale sweat overlaid
with Old Spice and Bovril.

Loud chatter, chants, laughter,
a buzz of excited energy
as, en masse, we emerge
among stands of plastic
blue seats, already half full
with yet more grown men.

I make my way to the front,
the standing-only area.
My nose is assailed with the scent
of freshly mown turf. My eyes
are overwhelmed by the ocean
of glistening green.

Twenty two men stepped out,
onto the pitch, royal blue
versus mustard yellow.
At the sound of a whistle
from a man, all in black,

they began to dance.

The Silkmen - Macclesfield Town Football Club, b.1874 – d.2020.

A Brief History

In 1988, under the leadership of Margaret Thatcher, the government updated the Local Government Act, to include Section 28.

Section 28 stated that local authorities **"shall not intentionally promote homosexuality or publish material with the intention of promoting homosexuality"** *, nor shall they **"promote the teaching in any maintained school of the acceptability of homosexuality as a pretended family relationship"** *.

This was finally repealed, after years of fighting by Stonewall (a UK charity for LGBTQ rights).
        In Scotland - 21st June 2000.
        In the rest of the UK - 18th November 2003.

From the Local Government Act 1988, Section 28

As someone who graduated in May 2000, Hannah was directly impacted by Section 28.

Shh

My fingers tingle with anticipation.
I close my eyes, scared that when I open them,
you'll have gone; it will have been a dream.
Numbness creeps up my arms,
my shoulders weaken with fear of the unknown.
We're told it's wrong, but it feels so, so right.
Our bodies lock like the key to my bike chain.
I want to wrap my arms around you
but I'm scared.

Scared of when to stop,
scared of what to do.

My toes have left me,
they're on the ceiling with
the rest of my body, watching you
touch me, caress my neck
with soft, damp lips.
Your lipstick leaves a mark,
tells the world what we're doing
in my bedroom, door locked,
parents at the supermarket.

I clasp my hands in yours, squeezing tight.
Your eyes hide secrets
and I'm scared.

Scared of where you are,
scared of repercussions.

I peel back your t-shirt,
and touch your belly
with the tips of my trembling fingers.

The tempo of my breath rises,
my fingers drip with nervous sweat.
As I struggle with the button on your jeans
your hands reach out and touch
my chest. I fear you'll feel my pounding
heart and stop.

But you smile and kiss my neck.
Your hands wander over my body,
stroking every crevice,
arousing every sense.

Gravel crunches outside the window
and we freeze
half climaxed, pause without breath.
Footsteps across the driveway,
a *click*, as the front door opens.
We unlock our bodies,
dive for our clothes,
red, flustered, silent.

Kneeling on the floor, we try to finish
our discarded game of Monopoly,
mutely agreeing
on our secret.

Keeping Mum

I can't tell a lie.
I can't keep a secret.
So the second I knew,
I had no choice,
it was an *itch*.

But what if
      she freaked out
And what if
      she was disgusted
What if
      she kicked me out,
      onto the streets,
      no bed, no food, no love

Or worse.

What if
      she sent me
      to live with my dad
What if
      she said she'd prefer to hear
      I was pregnant, or on drugs.
What if
      she didn't believe me,
      said it was 'just a phase'

'What if' makes food taste bland.
It turns your favourite tv show
into distant, incoherent mumblings.
It makes every song just noise
and the book you're reading
a blur of black lines.

'What if' makes your skin
feel detached from muscle and sinew.

'What if' will eventually kill you.

So, I interrupted her Monday night soaps
as she lay on the sofa,
head on my stepdad's lap,
feet curled up,
under her thick, woollen blanket.

I perched on the edge
of the armchair
and stared at them.
Sweat beads on my neck,
under my arms,
on my palms
and between my toes.
Wind blustered through my ears,
heart drumming, thrumming,
lips dry,
tongue dry.

"Mum, I need to tell you something."
She turned her gaze,
eyebrows raised, her mind
still on Hayley and Roy Cropper.

"Mum, I'm gay."

She smiled.
"Ok sweetheart."

Coming Out

They had no idea of the barrel
of festering maggots that question
represented. They didn't clock
the irony of interrogating me
during Religious Education.

Perhaps, if they had questioned me during English
I could have stood upon my desk
and poetically declared my unrequited
love for another girl.

Maybe, if they had probed me during Science,
I could have made the teacher
answer with a technical explanation
about how bees sometimes prefer other bees.

They should have quizzed me in Maths.
I would have used algebra
to show how $(y + y) - x =$ happiness.

The rumour was too tasty a titbit.
They couldn't wait, they insisted
they had a right to know;
PE was in the afternoon, see.

So I muttered yes,
because I cannot lie
and I sort-of-was, sort-of-am.

A Northern Changing Room

Oi.
Stop lookin'.
Miss… Miss, tell it.
Yer can't let *that* change in 'ere wi' us.
I'll get me mum in.
Disgusting.
Make it change wi' the boys.

Miss… Miss, it looked at Laura
when she were changin'.
Perv aren't yer.
I'm complainin'.
Not 'avin' this.

Miss… Miss, she said it 'erself -
she's *queer*,
she likes *girls*.
We're, like, vulnerable yer know.
She should be banned.
Me mum said so, last night.
And Becky's mum's already complained.

Miss… Miss, tell it.

An Ode

Sat, head bowed, neck bared,
my hand copying the phrases
as you wrote them on the whiteboard.

Sting

My pen jerked.
It's just a sting,
it won't leave a mark.
On the outside.

Sting, sting

I flinched, squeezed my eyelids
tight, gnashed my teeth, jaw set.
Just keep writing.

Sting, clink

Like a wasp bite.
Two pence weapon clattered
from my arm to the desk,
left a red welt.

You heard the words.
Queer, lezza, dyke.
I saw you flinch, mildly.
I saw you glance at me,
as my eyes screamed
stop them.

You turned your back.

Another coin hit my cheek.
The voices louder.
They saw you see me,
they saw you see my pain.
They saw.
They saw you condone it.

So I rose.
I wanted, so badly,
to punch, slap, stab, punish
the twenty smirking bullies.

Instead, I walked away.

You followed,
asked me to stay.
Only if you stop them.

You opened your mouth.
Closed it.
Opened it.
Don't you think, perhaps,
you brought this on yourself?

Law Be Damned

Another lesson with gritted teeth,
ice-cold, blank stares, flat lips.
Time to be emotionless.
I'd skive, but my love of learning
lures me in, my drive to be somebody,
someone wise, well read, well rounded.
I'm adamant they won't win.

I draw in the wind - fill my ears
with the sound of waves
crashing into rocks,
until it drowns the sounds
of insults and catcalling.

There is a line.
It might be invisible,
but it's there.
And he tripped over it
as he tipped
the contents of the bin
on my head.

As pencil shavings poured
through my blouse, into the gap
of my bra; as crumpled tissues
bounced off my head;
as a pen fell to my desk
and splattered ink on my book
I snapped.

Like a wolverine weasel,
I lunged for his face,
all claws and teeth.

You watched, from the sidelines,
paused while helping another student.

You stepped over,
touched my shoulder.
Calmed the rabid beast.
You spoke out.
Refused to condone.
Insisted on punishment
for him,
and help
for me.

Keep It Under Wraps

There goes my girlfriend
hanging with her friends,
giggling at cute boys
and discussing make-up tips.
No one knows a thing yet
because that's what she wants.

Walking by myself
trying to keep schtum.
Yearning to go to her,
to kiss her and say *hi*.

She wants to keep us quiet.
She wants me to tell no-one,
but meet her later on.

We'll go up to my bedroom,
listen to 70s punk and kiss
sweetly, just like other couples.

Her parents think we're friends,
best mates says her mum,
oblivious to our intimacy.

Keep it under wraps she whispers,
my mum's a homophobe.

Pride

It's easier if you're unpopular,
if you're mere entertainment for the masses.
The door's already unlocked,
you needn't fear the loss
of friends, when you don't have any.

So I shouted from the school roof,
with a bright red megaphone -
Damn straight, I am!

It doesn't hurt me when you yell *rug muncher*,
it doesn't sting when you spit out *dyke*.
I take those words and stitch them
on my bag as badges, next to the ones
that say "5ive are Number 1"
and "Nirvana 'til I die".

Because I didn't pander,
wasn't a sheep in your flock
coated in Number 7 foundation
and bright red nail varnish,
you obsessed over my bedroom antics
as much as Take That's break-up.

You even took the time to pause
and create a male nickname
for me. It had a song,
sang to the tune of the Haribo jingle.
Kids and grown-ups hate her so,
the dirty queer is Harry-B-O.

You wasted so much breath and thought
on the gobby little lesbian.

You tried to make me hate myself,
instead you made me prouder.

Those Days

At eight, did you want a curfew of nine pm,
so you could watch Casualty with your dad?
With fifty pence pocket money
did you spend an hour in the newsagents
torn between Beano and Dandy,
Snickers and Mars Bars?
As your birthday neared, did you calculate
the masses of extra sweets
a pay-rise would bring?
When it doubled to a pound
did you ask the shop lady
for a hundred fried eggs or ten chomps?

At twelve, did your mum promise
two pounds once you hit your teens?
Did you count the days 'til you could afford
Smash Hits instead of Quiz Kids?
Were you dreaming of your first kiss
and hugging your pillow
as though it was Mark Owen?
As you mum pulled away from the school gates,
did you pull out the lippy, hidden in your pencil case?

Did you, at thirteen, count your dinner money -
pricing chips, a bar of chocolate
and a crafty fag from the kid behind the tennis courts?
In sex-ed, were you shocked
to see a condom rolled onto a banana?
Or did you already know its texture and taste?
Was that you behind the bike sheds
locking lips with the recently expelled badboy?
Or did you creep through the gates,
hitching your skirt higher -

for your friends' older brother's best mate?

At fourteen did you keep a diary
filled with love hearts and 4evas?
Did you use initials only,
because your secret crush was a girl?
Were you stressing about exams,
cramming every spare minute
with equations and Hamlet quotes?
Or were you inhaling aerosols and nicotine,
kissing men and plotting
your escape route?

Did you lie on your bed
blasting Boyzone and 5ive
dreaming about marrying Leo?
Or was it Patti Smith and Placebo
while you sharpened a knife
and checked the Yellow Pages
for the nearest circus?

When you finally turned eighteen,
were you still at home peacefully
obeying rules? Or were you lying
on a moth eaten, piss-stained mattress,
with all the freedom you'd desired,
wishing you were eight,
with fifty pence to burn on comics?

These Days

(Not) Our Fight

Live for moments -
glorious goals, leg-stretching saves.

Panic over dramas -
fights for possession, triumph, trophies.

Watch from our armchairs,
beer and insults in hand,
edge of our seats, knuckles white.

Ninety minutes of heaven and hell.
Emotions rubbed raw, cut and bruised
heart – for the sake of success.

We scream better tactics,
beg for certain subs.
But we're miles away,
no influence at all.

Watch And Pray

See the modern dance on the holy-watered turf,
the yells and the pacing of the track-suited coach,
the oomph of the ball as it leaves a player's foot.
Praise for the keeper as he leaps like he's winged;
joyous in the crowd as, in unison, we sing.

This heart pumps with football, calcio, soccer, fùtbol;
tiki taka, gegenpress, Bielsaball, or park-the-bus.
The chips and the flicks, back passes, headers.
Goals from playmakers, strikers, full-backs;
last second scrambles, off-the-line clearances.

Match of the Day fanfare, Kris Kamara gaffes,
transfer speculations and youthful revelations.
Insane sums for unknown journeymen.
It's red versus blue, king versus country.
Dreams coming true when a team knows how to dance.

Time for the weekend ritual of praying to a ball.
Armchair is our prayer mat where we cry, cheer, jeer.
Living for the derby, the championship fights,
cup-winning nights and relegation plights.
We keep our faith – win, lose or draw.

Goodbye Silkmen

I watched your death from the sidelines.
As the whistle blew your death knell
I wept, sobbed, like I'd lost my brother.

I watched your death from the stands.
My heart broke. I stood, helpless,
as one man's greed took over.

I watched your death from another town,
from the doorstep of an opposing team
whose owners ran things properly.

A tax-grabbing cancer spread to your heart,
starved it's players of food and rent money,
signed a manager who could afford to wait.

Journalists warned us, like doctors
warn of a treatable brain tumour,
if operated on immediately.

Such arrogance and lack of love,
he refused to sell or pay his way.
So now we say goodbye.

No more days, sat in a sea
of blue and white joy
as we cheer you on,
encouraging goals and excellent saves.

No more cup nights,
where you stand toe-to-toe
with the big boys *eighty* spots higher;
where you concede early on,

but still win 2-1.

No more ecstasy or jubilation.
Just cold, hollow nights,
with floodlights turned off,
overgrown grass
and bittersweet memories.

Caus-Tic

I

To look back

is fright, a
dangerous plan.
Walking forward,
this blind,
is terror.

And so I close
my eyes, visualise
that day;
my mind
imploding.

II

Stashed down deep
memories ooze

seep.

And so it starts again,
this daily chore of pretence
and I,
a puppet show of joy.

The dam bursts,
a tsunami smothers
my smile.

The strings sag;
on bended knees
I crumble,
spent.

III

I cannot look back,
wallowing, writhing
a half-dead serpent.

I will let the artificial
serotonin flow through my veins.
I will look back

and bask in the pain
of learning, immerse myself
in the strength that took root

and grew.
A willow sapling,
drooping branches a shield.

In The Darkness

I do not see the world
through rose-tinted glasses.
I adore the thick blue-grey globs of rain
and the overcast mist
that clings to my neck,
that trickles down
my spine
like sweat.

Hazy, yellow-grey light
draws me in, moth-like.
Lost treasure I can find
without a map.
A pearl, or a gem.

Forest Hands

As foretold I succumbed
    blindfolded
        down the overgrown
forest path.
                so many roots
                              jut out
                try to trip me;
like snakes
    they slither
        across the path;
like tentacles
    they entwine
around my ankles;
    squeeze
        my bones
    yank me
        down
break my teeth,
  fill my mouth
with dust- soil- blood.

    Sometimes
I give in. Sometimes
        I let them
    lure me from the path.

There is a place
where mistakes
are insignificant -
a glade,
    to pause,
        to breathe,
to open my eyes,

blindfold untied.

I let in the sunlight,
	see the flutter
of crimson wings.

She rests on my shoulder,
Faery hands unknot the burr in my neck,
slay the muscle-biting gnats.

She steers me back, down
the glorious,
	terrifying
		forest path.

Autistic Sensibilities

So it seems
we're all unique.
So I'm told,
so I was raised.

So my quirkiness
shouldn't matter.

But it does.

Chatter itches,
ears can't focus
as the prattle, the noise
is now just me.
Inappropriate interruptions,
I can't still my tongue
until I release the words.

I can't read your face,
it's a blindness, you see.
The lights hurt,
too much movement
in my periphery.
Anxiety builds -
an active volcano.
Lava spurts, burns,
scalds those around me.

Now, I see.
I was never rude,
or invasive or mean.
I'm autistic, so please,
dim the lights

and forgive my formal tone.
I'm not patronising you,
I'm trying to be your friend.

Beauty in the Beast

Mosquitoes buzz and pierce our flesh,
hungry. Fire ants sting and bite,
an army's picnic for veteran ex-pats.
We, their feast, can merely scratch
the flaming rash and swollen skin.

Transported from the pain,
the incessant itching,
swim gentle backstrokes
in the ocean. Eyes shut,
bright sunlight cuts
through eyelids too thin
to hide our imagination -
where the hawk soars over untold
stories of foot-soldier faeries,
carnivorous mermaids, cowering
trolls and sentient spicy saffron.

The water sparkles, glitters,
as we drift on our back,
ears filling with muffled,
waterlogged silence.

Skin soothed, let us stroll along
our beach, sandy shore
at the mouth of our cave.
Micro-lives moulded like clay
into this haven of limestone.
Sun-bleached and salt-water soaked,
the rocks glisten as Poseidon's roar
thrashes waves, a hypnotic
shower of fearsome nature.

Lean back, nestle into the cold,
jagged rock. Embrace the sharp
solidity. Take a shell, a conch,
raise it to freshly soothed ears
and listen to the purr of the dragon
as he sleeps a slumber so deep
he will twitch taloned claws,
lip trembling over his deadly teeth,
tantalising you into stroking
his iridescent blue scales.

Fearless, we can rest, enveloped
by our sinuous serpentine guardian.

Less Judging

Shift our gaze
from anti to pro;
avert our eyes
from fascists on both sides.

To Your Right

Such freedom given -
civilisation democratised.

A century of progression
crammed into a decade.

Unexpected evolution
takes longer
than humans can handle.

No surprise
when the fascist volcano

      erupts,

spews white-hot racist slurs;
murdered innocents stream down
the side
of our world;

blackens sunlight
with the dense steam
of homophobia.

Fear of change and the
unknown. Acidic ignorance

      rains

on our liberal cheeks.

Impossible Politics

how many words does it take
to draw a picture
how many chickens does it take
to fly a plane
how many paddles does it take
a car to move

how many journalists
does it take to read the news
how many meteorologists
does it take to see the storm
How many politicians
does it take to fuck the world?

Silicon Era

Such a glorious revolution -
this silicon valley of joy.

Apple and YouTube, Google and Yahoo,
iPad, Xbox, laptop and smartphone;
flatscreen, 4k, 3D beauty;
in a house of gadgets,
boredom is extinct.

A cloud of data from our Amazon purchases;
personalised adverts to make us feel special,
they dub your name into adverts
and invade Facebook-mooching.

The world is watching so we flaunt our faces.
Social Media: no degree needed,
just a pretty trout-pout and Instagram filters.

Gaming is a sport now.
Multicoloured flashing lights,
an 80s rave without the pills.
Sat on leather thrones,
caressing their control pads,
teams of gamers
with teems of followers.

As we drive through the cloud,
Alexa as co-pilot,
we heed views not facts
from genderless avatars.
These warriors sit at desks,
their keyboard is their sword,
so we knight them Sir Troll.

They click, the mouse a trigger,
gunning down minorities
for daring to think differently.

Yet still we kneel feeling blessed,
thinking Digital is God
and we are its Kings.

Flight

Our dragon soars over forests of war;
we cling to her scales, vibrate from her roars.
Smell the sulphur engulf us as clouds
open fire, acid rain melting
through aeroplanes and drones
that attack with dictatorship,
hatred and fear.

Religious fervour wears eau-de-murder.
Vitamin Pain drip-feeds our future.
Children rotting, limbs detached;
innocent heads hanging from trees.
Women weep, violated, haunted,
praying for death's hand
to erase their torment.

Our blood boils and roils, seeps into our steed.
With thunderous rumbles, she swoops
down on the scene, the massacre, the bloodbath;
spits fire at the beasts that demolish our peace;
tears them to ribbons with claws glistening red;
crunches on bones with sabre-sharp fangs.

Redundant revenge,
we tremble with rage.
We swallow the suffering,
gulp down injustice.
Our mouths overflowing
with futility and hope.

Forsaken

Full of hatred, discrimination,
buzzing from the power
of your guns and tasers -
you make judgement calls
as though you have the right
to say who lives or dies.

I see you,
we see you,
as you pick off our Black friends
like your ancestors did.
You stomp through lives
like you're above all others.
You kneel on necks,
choke-hold innocents,
ignore pleas for help,
for a simple
        breath.

The cycle goes on
without you learning.
You deny this world's true
history; implant it with lies
that paint you as the best,
the only, the supreme.

Centuries of blood shed
as you stomped across the globe
sticking flags in the earth
like you did to the moon.
You landed on far-flung shores,
welcomed by Natives,
offered trade, gifts and love.

But you pierced their trust
with swords, muskets and arrogance.

You stand on their bones,
dehumanise their pain,
devalue their lives.
You crush hope
like weeds in the cracks
of your concrete patio.

But they are wild roses,
and we are their thorns.
Their roots have entwined
beneath the soil of our dead.

Summer has come,
the flowers are erupting,
blossoming, alive.

Crown of Thorns

Stand over there, wait your turn.
We're in this together, dominoes
placed in the shape of a white flag.

I see your panic, I smell your fear.
The wolf approaches, hackles raised,
bristled thorny fur, glistening
fangs bared, dripping blood;
a deathly crown upon his ferocious head.

Please step back: It's time.
A cloak of invisibility hides
the sight of teeth on innocent flesh.
Use this microscope to see
he kills without prejudice, reason or rhyme.

Stop acting blasé, I beg you
heed the countless professionals
who stare down the beast;
they're not crying wolf
they are *screaming* it.

These Days

We surf a wave of bacterial power,
felled by something unseen
as it sneaks into our lungs,
clings to the tiny hairs
and steals our breath.

We duck, dodge, weave
a barrage of hatred.
Vitriolic leaders stoke the fire,
tweet nastiness and falsehoods,
divert the attention of us peasants.

Neighbour turns on neighbour,
brother turns on uncle.
Facts are left unread,
but fake news is dog-eared,
covered in the thumb prints of millions.

People beheaded for teaching free speech,
while those preaching hate speech
are lauded, revered.

LGBT-free zones,
that scream *we'll kill you
if you're queer*.

Progression in reverse
is a nightmare to behold.
Friend turns on friend,
mother turns on sister.
This civil war is a global pandemic.

Just one little thought,

taught when we're young:
We can disagree
but I don't hate you.

About the author

Hannah Edge is a 36 year old poet based in the Midlands, England; surrounded by 70s terraces, rundown high streets, and secret pockets of luscious willow trees, woodland paths and lakes.

She has been writing poetry since she was a 6, when she would split her time between reading everything she could lay her hands on – from books to shampoo bottles, and writing on everything she could lay her hands on – her parent's huge 90s computer, toilet paper, her own body, the walls, and sometimes even with plain ol' paper.

She has self-identified as a poet since the age of 16, when she was first published (Girl 2 Girl – a Diva Magazine anthology). Not long after, she attained a BA(Hons) in Imaginative Writing, where she focused primarily on her poetry and discovered a love of prose. During this time her poetry and short stories featured in Poetry Pool 3, In The Red and Little Giants Magazine.

Hannah then spent a decade travelling, exploring her mental health and sexuality, marrying and divorcing. In 2019, she found the courage to show the world her poetry again. She was shortlisted for the 2019 National Poetry Day #speakyourtruth competition with her poem, Autistic Sensibilities. Since then, she has been writing ferociously, like the 6 year old she remembers; finding joy in language, emotion and memories.

Hannah can be found online at:

Twitter: edge_hannah

Insta: observeandmuse_ehjee

Facebook: https://www.facebook.com/hannah.edgeynwa

Facebook page: ObserveandMuse

Poetry Blog: observemuseedge.wordpress.com